CELEBRATING THE FAMILY NAME OF ELLIOTT

Celebrating the Family Name of Elliott

Walter the Educator

Silent King Books
a WhichHead Entertainment Imprint

Copyright © 2024 by Walter the Educator

All rights reserved. No part of this book may be reproduced in any manner whatsoever without written permission except in the case of brief quotations embodied in critical articles and reviews.

First Printing, 2024

Disclaimer

This book is a literary work; the story is not about specific persons, locations, situations, and/or circumstances unless mentioned in a historical context. Any resemblance to real persons, locations, situations, and/or circumstances is coincidental. This book is for entertainment and informational purposes only. The author and publisher offer this information without warranties expressed or implied. No matter the grounds, neither the author nor the publisher will be accountable for any losses, injuries, or other damages caused by the reader's use of this book. The use of this book acknowledges an understanding and acceptance of this disclaimer.

Celebrating the Family Name of Elliott is a memory book that belongs to the Celebrating Family Name Book Series by Walter the Educator. Collect them all and more books at WaltertheEducator.com

USE THE EXTRA SPACE TO DOCUMENT YOUR FAMILY MEMORIES THROUGHOUT THE YEARS

ELLIOTT

The name of Elliott, proud and strong,

A family bound by story and song.

Through years that stretch, through tales untold,

They carry dreams both bright and bold.

With roots that deepen, firm and wide,

The Elliotts stand with strength and pride.

In fields of green or city's sprawl,

They rise as one, they heed the call.

Each Elliott heart, both fierce and kind,

Is built of grit and thoughtful mind.

Through trials met and battles faced,

They hold their name with quiet grace.

In laughter rich and voices clear,

They lift each other, year by year.

With steady hands and visions bright,

They seek the truth, they find the light.

Through storms of life, they hold their way,

.

With courage born anew each day.

In every challenge, every feat,

The Elliott spirit won't retreat.

Their hands are strong, their hearts sincere,

They build a world both close and near.

In acts of love, in bonds so tight,

They find their strength, they shine their light.

Through ties of kin that will not break,

In all they give and all they make,

They weave a tale that's strong and true,

A legacy both old and new.

In every voice, in every song,

They find the place where they belong.

With every dream, with every choice,

The Elliott name, a steadfast voice.

With gentle grace and fiery might,

They face the dawn, they chase the night.

For love and honor, fierce and free,

They live as one, a family tree.

So here's to Elliott, brave and bright,

A name that fills both day and night.

With strength and love, they make their way,

The Elliott light, come what may.

ABOUT THE CREATOR

Walter the Educator is one of the
pseudonyms for Walter Anderson.
Formally educated in Chemistry,
Business, and Education, he is an
educator, an author, a diverse
entrepreneur, and he is the son
of a disabled war veteran.
"Walter the Educator" shares his
time between educating and creating.
He holds interests and owns several
creative projects that entertain,
enlighten, enhance, and educate,
hoping to inspire and motivate you.
Follow, find new works, and stay
up to date with Walter the Educator™

at WaltertheEducator.com

Milton Keynes UK
Ingram Content Group UK Ltd.
UKHW021627011224
451755UK00010B/492

9 798330 577347